THE ARMPIT OF DOOM

Funny Poems for Kids

D0104477

Kenn Nesbitt

Illustrations by
Rafael Domingos

Published by
Purple Room Publishing
1314 S Grand Blvd #2-321
Spokane, Washington 99202

Fax: 815-642-8206

www.poetry4kids.com

For Easton and Isaac

Contents

The Armpit of Doom

Today I walked into my big brother's room,
and that's when I saw it: The Armpit of Doom.
I wasn't expecting The Armpit at all.
I shrieked and fell backward and grabbed for the wall.
The Armpit was smelly. The Armpit was hairy.
The Armpit was truly disgusting and scary.
I wanted to vomit. I wanted to cry.
I wanted to flee from its all-seeing eye.
My skin started crawling with goose bumps and chills.
My brain began screaming to head for the hills.
I tried to escape but I knew I could not.
In horror, I found I was glued to the spot.

"Will somebody help me!?" I started to shout,
till fumes overcame me and made me pass out.
And that's why I'm here in this hospital room;
it's all on account of The Armpit of Doom.
I'm still feeling shaken. I'm queasy and pale,
but lucky I lived and can tell you my tale.
So take my advice… If you ever go near
your big brother's room, bring a whole lot of gear:
A gas mask and goggles, a helmet and shield,
or maybe a space suit that's perfectly sealed.
And then, only then, when you're fully prepared,
step in very slowly and hope you'll be spared.
But, if you're afraid of the Armpit of Doom,
stay far, far away from your big brother's room.

Please Don't Read this Poem

Please don't read this poem.
It's only meant for me.
That's it. Just move along now.
There's nothing here to see.

Besides, I'm sure you'd rather
just go outside and play.
So put the poem down now
and slowly back away.

Hey, why are you still reading?
That isn't very nice.
I've asked you once politely.
Don't make me ask you twice.

I'm telling you, it's private.
Do not read one more line.
Hey! That's one more. Now stop it.
This isn't yours; it's mine.

You're not allowed to read this.
You really have to stop.
If you don't quit this instant,
I swear I'll call a cop.

He'll drag you off in handcuffs.
He'll lock you up in jail,
and leave you there forever
until you're old and frail.

Your friends will all forget you.
You won't be even missed.
Your family, too, will likely
forget that you exist.

And all because you read this
instead of having fun.
It's too late now, amigo;
the poem's nearly done.

There's only one solution.
Here's what you'll have to do:
Tell all your friends and family
they shouldn't read it too.

My Brother's Not a Werewolf

My brother's not a werewolf
though it often looks that way.
He has to shave his whiskers
almost every single day.

His feet are getting furry
and his hands are sprouting hair.
His voice is deep and growling
like a grumpy grizzly bear.

He often sleeps throughout the day
and stays up half the night.
And if you saw the way he eats
you'd surely scream in fright.

His clothes are ripped and dirty
like the stuff a werewolf wears.
His socks and shirts are shredded
and his pants have countless tears.

If you should ever meet him
you'll discover what I mean.
My brother's not a werewolf;
he's just turning seventeen.

My Pet Germs

I have about a billion germs
I keep as tiny pets.
They're cute and clean and never mean
and give me no regrets.

They spend all day engaged in play
upon my skin and hair.
They're on my clothes, between my toes
and in my underwear.

They dance and shout and bounce about.
They run and jump and slide.
My epidermis teems with germs
who party on my hide.

I never fret about the pets
inside my shirt and socks.
I love them there but wonder where
they keep their litter box?

My Parents Sent Me to the Store

My parents sent me to the store
to buy a loaf of bread.
I came home with a puppy
and a parakeet instead.

I came home with a guinea pig,
a hamster and a cat,
a turtle and a lizard
and a friendly little rat.

I also had a monkey
and a mongoose and a mouse.
Those animals went crazy
when I brought them in the house.

They barked and yelped and hissed
and chased my family out the door.
My parents never let me
do the shopping anymore.

Our Teacher Sings the Beatles

Our teacher sings The Beatles.
She must know every song.
We ask her please to stop
but she just sings, "It Won't Be Long."

And then she croons like Elvis.
She clearly thinks it's cool.
And if we beg her not to
she just belts out, "Don't be Cruel."

She then does Michael Jackson.
It drives us nearly mad.
We have to cover up our ears
because she's singing, "Bad."

She winds up with The Wiggles
or else a Barney song,
and, even worse, she tells us all
that we should sing along.

It's all my fault she does this.
I feel like such a fool.
I wish I'd never brought
my karaoke box to school.

Mr. Brown the Circus Clown

Mr. Brown, the circus clown
puts his clothes on upside down.
He wears his hat upon his toes
and socks and shoes upon his nose.

He ties his ties around his thighs
and wraps his belt around his eyes.
He hangs his earrings from his hips
and stockings from his fingertips.

He puts his glasses on his feet
and shirt and coat around his seat.
And when he's dressed, at last he stands
and walks around upon his hands.

On the Thirty-Third of Januaugust

On the thirty-third of Januaugust,
right before Octember,
a strange thing didn't happen
that I always won't remember.

At eleven in the afternoon,
while making midnight brunch,
I poured a glass of sandwiches
and baked a plate of punch.

Then I climbed up on my head to see
the silver sky of green,
and danced around my feet because
I'd turned eleventeen.

A parade began to end
and music started not to play,
as rain came out and snowed all night
that warm and sunny day.

That was how it didn't happen
as I keenly don't remember,
on the thirty-third of Januaugust,
right before Octember.

Happy Birthday

I've got a lot of presents
that I'd like to give to you.
I'll give you all my Brussels sprouts
and all my liver too.

I'll give you all my gym socks
when they really start to stink.
I'll give you all my pens when
they are running out of ink.

I'll give you all my broken toys
and empty jars of paste.
I'll give you all my bubble gum
that's chewed and lost its taste.

I'll give you all the dust balls that
I found beneath my bed.
I'll give you all my batteries
as soon as they are dead.

So have a happy birthday,
you're a special friend indeed,
and please accept this trashcan
full of stuff that I don't need.

I'm Practically Perfect

I'm practically perfect in every respect.
I haven't a flaw you could ever detect.
As soon as you know me I'm sure you'll agree
there's no one around who's as perfect as me.

I'm handsome and rich, with a generous heart.
I'm funny and charming and totally smart.
At school, in my classes, I only get A's.
I'm also athletic in so many ways.

My clothes are expensive. My hair is just right.
My teeth are all straight, and they're shiny and white.
I'm practically perfect. I'm sure you could tell.
And, oh, did I mention? I'm humble as well.

That Explains It!

I went to the doctor. He x-rayed my head.
He stared for a moment and here's what he said.
"It looks like you've got a banana in there,
an apple, an orange, a peach, and a pear.

I also see something that looks like a shoe,
a plate of spaghetti, some fake doggy doo,
an airplane, an arrow, a barrel, a chair,
a salmon, a camera, some old underwear,
a penny, a pickle, a pencil, a pen,
a hairy canary, a hammer, a hen,
a whistle, a thistle, a missile, a duck,
an icicle, bicycle, tricycle, truck.
With all of the junk that you have in your head,
it's kind of amazing you got out of bed.
The good news, at least, is you shouldn't feel pain.
From what I can see here you don't have a brain."

Electronic Christmas

I asked for new gadgets for Christmas.
My list was a hundred lines long.
I figured I might as well try it.
Why not? I mean, what could go wrong?

My parents bought all that I wanted:
An iPod, a big-screen TV,
a camera, a laptop computer,
a PlayStation, Xbox, and Wii.

I got a new Kindle, a smart phone,
an RF remote-controlled car,
a robot, a video camera,
a brand new electric guitar.

But those things were just the beginning.
This Christmas I had such a haul,
it took me all morning, and then some,
to finish unwrapping it all.

A hundred new gadgets to play with.
I couldn't be bothered to wait.
The moment I plugged them all in, though,
it blew every fuse in the state.

If you're spending Christmas in darkness,
and can't play your video game,
I'm sorry for all of the trouble;
it's probably me who's to blame.

I know now I shouldn't be greedy,
so, next year, I think you'll be fine.
Instead of a hundred new gadgets,
I'm asking for just ninety nine.

Broccoli for Breakfast

Broccoli for breakfast.
Broccoli for lunch.
Broccoli that's tender.
Broccoli with crunch.

Broccoli for dinner.
Broccoli for snacks.
Broccoli in boxes
and baskets and sacks.

Broccoli for weeks and
for months and for years.
It's up to my eyeballs.
It's up to my ears!

I used to like broccoli
but now, I'm afraid,
its beauty, at best,
is beginning to fade.

It's lacking in luster.
It's lost all its charm.
But that's how it goes
on a broccoli farm.

Octoproblem

My teacher said to calculate
3.141 times 8.
I threw my hand up instantly
and so, of course, she called on me.
She asked me, "What's the answer, please?"
I'd figured this one out with ease.
I looked her squarely in the eye
and calmly answered, "Octopi!"
It took her half an hour to get it,
and then she gave me extra credit.

Gilman Glum

When Gilman Glum would suck his thumb,
he'd claim, "It's just the best!
It's simply incontestable.
I've put it to the test.

"I've sucked the thumbs of kings and queens,
of presidents and popes.
I've sucked the thumbs of geniuses
and even those of dopes.

"The taste is so delectable.
No other thumb compares.
I've tried the thumbs of beggared bums
and multi-millionaires.

"I've tasted thumbs from far away
and thumbs from right next door;
from San Francisco, Santa Fe,
and even Singapore.

"I tried a few from Kathmandu
and Norway and Nepal.
Yes, when it comes to sucking thumbs
I'm sure I've tried them all.

"If ever you could try it too
I'm sure that you'd agree.
But, sadly though you'll never know;
my thumb is just for me."

Bubble Wrap, Bubble Wrap

Bubble wrap, bubble wrap,
pop, pop, pop.
Wrapped around my bottom.
Wrapped around my top.

I'm double-wrapped in bubble wrap
It's covering my clothes.
It's wrapped around my fingers.
It's wrapped around my toes.

I've wrapped myself in bubble wrap
exactly as I'd planned.
But now I'm tied so tightly,
I can barely even stand.

I'm having trouble walking.
I can hardly even hop.
I guess I'll have to roll today.
Pop, pop, pop.

When Frankenstein Was Just a Kid

When Frankenstein was just a kid,
he ate his greens. It's true. He did!
He ate his spinach, salads, peas,
asparagus, and foods like these.
And with each leaf and lima bean
his skin became a bit more green.

On chives and chard he loved to chew,
and Brussels sprouts and peppers too,
until he ate that fateful bean
that turned his skin completely green.
He turned all green, and stayed that way,
and now he frightens folks away.

Poor Frankenstein, his tale is sad,
but things need not have been so bad.
It's fair to say, if only he
had eaten much less celery,
avoided cabbage, ate no kale,
why, then, we'd have a different tale.

And that is why I'm here to say
please take these vegetables away
or my fate could be just as grim.
Yes, I could end up green like him.
So, mom and dad, before we dine,
please give a thought to Frankenstein.

I Never Want to Go to Bed

I never want to go to bed.
I like to stay up late.
I'm bouncing off the bedroom walls
and, frankly, feeling great!

I'm dancing like a maniac
instead of counting sheep.
My mom says, "Time for bed."
My dad yells, "Get your butt to sleep!"

I'm not sure what my bottom
has to do with anything,
but that's okay because I'd rather
jump around and sing.

I don't know what it was
that made me feel so wide awake.
Could it have been the Red Bull
and the double-chocolate cake?

I wonder if the seven cups
of coffee plus dessert
of Hershey bars and Skittles
are what left me this alert?

Whatever it turns out to be
that made me feel this right,
I hope I track it down
so I can stay up every... *ZZZzzzzz*

Digging for Diamonds

I'm digging for diamonds.
I'm digging for gold.
I'm digging for silver
that's shiny and cold.

I'm digging all day and
I'm digging all night.
I'm digging for rubies
all sparkling and bright.

I plan to get famous.
I plan to get rich
by digging up gemstones
in ditch after ditch.

And yet, from these ditches
I've dug in the ground,
there weren't any diamonds
or coins to be found.

I haven't got silver
or rubies, you see...
I just have my mom and dad
yelling at me.

For though I found nothing
from digging till dawn,
my parents found holes
where we once had a lawn.

The Tall Tale of Shorty Small

Shorty Small
was very tall
despite his humble name.
In fact, his height
was quite a sight,
and Shorty's claim to fame.

Yes, Shorty Small
was so, so tall,
to reach to brush his hair,
he'd have to climb,
for quite some time,
a ladder way up there.

To tie his shoes,
he had to use
a rope or knotted sheet
to clamber down
toward the ground
to even reach his feet.

And that is all
of Shorty Small
that's worthy to report.
For, overall,
although he's tall,
his tale is rather short.

I'll Never

I'll never climb Mount Everest
to see what I can see.
I'll never be the President
by popular decree.
I'll never rule the jungle
with my trusted chimpanzee.
I'll never rustle cattle
with a friend named Tennessee.

I'll never work with Sherlock Holmes
to solve a tricky case.
I'll never fly a fighter jet
and be a flying ace.
I'll never run a marathon
and break the record pace.
I'll never ride a rocket ship
to float in outer space.

I'll never run away
to join the Legionnaires in France.
I'll never play on Broadway
as a master of the dance.
I'll never joust on horseback
with a helmet and a lance.
I'll never win a million
in a lucky game of chance.

I'll never woo a princess
in the hills of Kathmandu.
I'll never win an Oscar
for my Hollywood debut.
My list is long of all the things
I know I'll never do
because I'd rather watch TV.
Is that how you are too?

The Toughest Pastry Maker

I'm the toughest pastry maker
who has ever baked a cake.
My impressive little pastries
are impossible to break.
Yes, my cookies and my cupcakes
will defeat the strongest jaws,
while my muffins are impervious
to power drills and saws.

You have never seen a danish
or a donut quite so strong
and I bake the fiercest fruitcake
that has ever come along.
You can chew on them till doomsday,
you can chew till kingdom come,
but you'll never get a nibble,
not a solitary crumb.

You can whack them with a hammer,
you can hit them with a stick.
You can stab them with a dagger,
you can beat them with a brick.
You can drop them from an airplane,
you can blast them with a bomb,
but my pastries will exhibit only
peacefulness and calm.

I expect you'll want to test them.
I encourage you to try,
but you'll never make a mark on them
and here's the reason why:
I do something with my recipes
no other bakers do;
when the cookbook calls for "milk" or "water,"
I use Crazy Glue.

I'm Thankful for Turkey

I'm thankful for turkey.
I'm thankful for yams.
I'm thankful for cranberries,
biscuits, and hams.

I'm thankful for pumpkins.
I'm thankful for cheese.
I'm thankful for gravy,
potatoes, and peas.

I'm thankful for stuffing;
I'm nuts for the stuff.
I'm thankful for eggnog
and marshmallow fluff.

I'm thankful for whipped cream
and ice cream and pies.
I'm thankful for dad's
double-chocolate surprise.

I'm thankful, Thanksgiving,
for good things to eat.
But mostly I'm thankful
I still see my feet.

Pansy P. Petunia

I'm Pansy P. Petunia
and I never take a shower.
There isn't any need because
I smell just like a flower.

My breath smells like forget-me-nots.
My burps smell like impatiens.
My armpits smell like daisies
and my feet smell like carnations.

But what is most impressive
and should tickle many noses
is every time I "cut the cheese"
it makes me smell like roses.

But maybe I'm mistaken
and could use a bath today,
since everyone who smells me
holds their nose and runs away!

It'sFuntoLeavetheSpacesOut

It'sfuntoleavethespacesout
ofeverythingyouwrite.
Topackyourwordstogether
isanabsolutedelight.

Atfirstitmayseemhardtodo,
but,afterjustawhile,
you'llfindyoulikecomposing
inthiscleanandcompactstyle.

Andeveryonewhoseesyourwords
willmarvelatyourskill.
They'lltellyouthattoreadyourwork
issomethingofathrill.

Andyou'llbecomesofamous
forthecleverwayyouwrite
thatyoucouldoutsellJ.K.Rowling
almostovernight.

Andsoonyou'llbeamillionaire;
ofthis,there'slittledoubt,
wheneveryotherbookyousee
looks t o t a l l y   s p a c e d   o u t.

I Knew a Guy

I knew a guy
who knew a guy
who stuck his finger
in his eye.
Oh me, oh my!
That silly guy!
He stuck his finger
in his eye!
I asked him, "Why,
oh tell me why
you stuck your finger
in your eye."

But all that guy
would do was cry
and cry and cry
and cry and cry.
So stick your finger
in a pie
or in the sky
or on your tie
or on a toasted
ham on rye
or on a purple
butterfly
but don't be like
that silly guy
who stuck his finger
in his eye
or you will cry
and cry and cry
and then you might
fall down and die.
Goodbye.

To Learn to Juggle Prickly Pears

To learn to juggle prickly pears
can take a lot of practice.
It takes a thousand shrieks and swears
to learn to juggle cactus.

Just try to juggle porcupines!
You're guaranteed to scream.
Anemones with all their spines
are equally extreme.

To stop the painful pokes and stings
you must get metal mittens
or else just juggle fluffy things.
That's why I juggle kittens.

The Bagel Bird

The Bagel Bird, by all accounts,
is said to lunch on large amounts
of sticks and twigs and sand and stones
and plastic parts from broken phones.
He'll nibble bits of copper wires
and rubber from discarded tires.
He'll chomp on tops of cuckoo clocks
and swallow shorts and stinky socks.

He'll chew your shoes and eat your hat.
He'll bite your books and baseball bat.
He'll stuff his lips with poker chips
and snack on sails from sailing ships
and gobble poles and bowling balls
and pick at bricks from fallen walls
and graze on grass and feed on weeds
and dine on twine and strings of beads.

But bagels... whether white or wheat,
or salted, savory, or sweet,
or topped with lox or luncheon meat,
are something he will never eat.
At least that's what I've always heard
about the crazy Bagel Bird.
But I don't mind because, you see,
that leaves more bagels just for me.

Benjamin Plays Bass Guitar

Benjamin plays bass guitar
completely out of tune.
Sarah sings while sucking from
a helium balloon.

Payton plays piano with her
elbows and her chin.
Brayden bangs on buckets
with a plastic bowling pin.

Nathan's nose has two kazoos;
one sharp, the other flat.
Bailey sits on bagpipes
sounding like a screaming cat.

We play this way on purpose
with a sound no one can stand.
It's fun to be the country's most
annoying student band.

Melvin the Mummy

Melvin the mummy, who lived near the Nile,
had worked as a mummy for more than a while,
for mummies can go their entire careers
without a vacation for thousands of years.

He guarded the pyramids day after day
to frighten the burglars and bandits away,
which meant, as he stood watching over the pharaohs,
he often got shot at with bullets and arrows.

His job was so stressful, the pay was so poor,
but, still, Melvin stayed and protected the door
until he got sick of his sad situation
and knew that he needed to take a vacation.

His crypt was so dark and so cold and so clammy,
he packed up his swimsuit and flew to Miami.
He thought he would stay there for just a few days,
enjoying the beach and absorbing some rays.

But, sadly, poor Melvin would never return,
and this is a lesson all mummies should learn:
Don't take any trips or, like Melvin, you'll find
vacations make mummies relax and unwind.

I Grew a Foot This Summer

I grew a foot this summer
and I wish it wasn't true.
I'm not twelve inches taller,
I just need an extra shoe.

Bouncing off the Windows

I'm bouncing off the windows.
I'm bouncing off the walls.
I'm feeling like my feet are made
of bouncing rubber balls.

I'm running like I'm crazy.
I'm running like I'm mad.
I might look like a lunatic
but, boy, I'm feeling glad.

I'm jumping like a kangaroo
or like a jumping bean.
I act this way at least a week
right after Halloween.

When Larry Made Lasagna

When Larry made lasagna
all his neighbors stopped and stared.
His lasagna was the largest
that had ever been prepared.

He used ninety yards of pasta
and a half a ton of cheese,
and the sauce, he spread with spatulas
that looked a lot like skis.

With a hundred pounds of vegetables
and wagon-loads of meat
plus a tiny sprig of parsley
his lasagna was complete.

So he lifted that lasagna
with a forklift and a crane
and he placed it in an oven
that was longer than a train.

For a week, while it was baking,
its aroma filled the town.
Then he took it from the oven,
piping hot and golden brown.

All the neighbors watched and waited
as he tasted it, and then
he explained, "I think it needs more salt.
I'll have to start again."

I'm Growing a Truck in the Garden

I'm growing a truck in the garden.
It's true, though it may sound bizarre.
I'm growing a bus and an airplane,
a rocket, a boat, and a car.

I planted them yesterday morning.
I'm sure they'll be sprouting up soon.
I'll water them all every morning,
and care for them each afternoon.

My mother said, "Let's plant a garden,"
for gardens are one of her joys,
but I didn't have any plant seeds
so that's why I planted my toys.

I Raised My Hand in Class

I raised my hand in class this morning,
sitting in the back.
The teacher didn't see, I think.
Instead she called on Jack.

I stretched my hand up higher,
but she called on Zach and Zoe.
I started bouncing up and down,
but, still, she called on Chloe.

I waved my arms but, even so,
she didn't call on me.
She called on Bryan, Brooklyn, Billy,
Bailey, Ben, and Bree.

She called on Taylor, Tristan, Thomas,
Trinity, and Ty.
Then, finally, she called my name.
I breathed a heavy sigh.

She asked me for the answer.
I just frowned and clenched my knees,
and said, "I've no idea,
but could I use the bathroom, please?"

Nathaniel Naste

Nathaniel Naste
once ate some paste
he'd taken home from school.
He scooped a bit
and tasted it
and hollered like a fool.
His face got laced
with paste that graced
his forehead and his hair.
Some paste got placed
upon his waist
which glued him to his chair.

Nathaniel cried
and, mortified,
his mother came to see.
She tugged, she tried,
she pulled and pried,
but couldn't get him free.
For she was stuck
in pasty muck
and called Nathaniel's dad,
who raced in haste,
embraced the paste,
and pulled with all he had.

But father too
was stuck like glue
to poor Nathaniel's mother,
and it ensued
they also glued
his sister and his brother,
his cat, his frog,
his bird, his dog
(a parakeet and spaniel),
till each at last
were fastened fast,
cemented to Nathaniel.

The neighbors came
and soon the same
was happening to all.
They faced the paste
but soon, disgraced,
they placed an urgent call
to nine-one-one
and on the run
came firemen and police,
who tried with ropes
and prayers and hopes
and bucket-loads of grease.

But nothing helped
and each one yelped
to be in this position
encased in paste
to find they faced
a sticky proposition.
Across the floor
and out the door
and halfway down the street,
with knees on hips,
and hands on lips,
and elbows stuck to feet.

The Army marched
but soon were starched.
The Navy gummed their ships.
The Air Force flew
but stuck like glue
to all those knees and lips.
The President
gave his consent
for every single person
to lend some aid
but this just made
the situation worsen.

And in the end
it's true, my friend,
no solitary granule
of any worth
was left on Earth
not pasted to Nathaniel.
So don't you fail
to heed this tale
and never taste your paste,
or you may find
you're in a bind
Like poor Nathaniel Naste.

I Wrote an Awful Poem

I wrote an awful poem;
it was bad in the extreme.
I showed it to my sister
and it made my sister scream.

I gave it to my mother
and she promptly flipped her lid.
My father blew a gasket,
and my baby brother hid.

I brought my poem with me
when I came to school today.
My teacher nearly fainted
and my friends all ran away.

I never knew a poem could be
such amazing fun.
But that was just a blast,
I think I'll write another one.

For My Brother, On His Birthday

For my brother, on his birthday,
I was generous and kind.
As his sister, I was glad to get
the best things I could find.

I was sure he'd want a tutu
and a purple mini-skirt,
with some ballerina slippers
and a sequin-covered shirt.

I expected he'd want lots of dolls.
I knew he'd need a bike,
so I picked a pink and sparkly one
I figured he would like.

I selected a tiara
like a princess ought to wear,
plus a bunch of bows and ribbons
and some scrunchies for his hair.

I'm aware I'm much too generous
with presents but, you see,
he deserves it; on my birthday
he bought baseball cards for me.

Rudy Tude

Rudy Tude is rather rude.
There's no one half as mean.
He truly is the crudest dude
that anyone has seen.

He'll poke you in the eye for fun.
He'll step upon your toes.
He'll yell at you until you run,
then spray you with a hose.

He'll wipe his nose upon his sleeves.
He'll spit upon the ground.
So everybody always leaves
when Rudy Tude's around.

And, all alone, he'll sit and cry
but never make amends.
He'll only cry and wonder why
he hasn't any friends.

Riding a Rainbow

I'll ride on a rainbow
to soar through the sky.
I'll ride on a kite
as it flies way up high.

I'll ride on a dragon.
I'll ride a balloon.
I'll ride on a rocket
and ride on the moon.

I'll ride on the wind
and the sun and the stars,
on floating bananas
and flying guitars.

I'll ride on a cloud
and a unicorn too.
I'll ride in the seat
of a magical shoe.

But why would I ride
on the sun and the stars?
It's so much more fun
than just riding in cars.

I Ran for the Chapstick

I ran for the Chapstick mom keeps in her purse.
My lips were so chapped that they couldn't feel worse!
I dug through her handbag and pulled it out quickly,
then sighed in relief as I smeared it on thickly.
I felt so much better I almost rejoiced.
My painful, dry lips were now mended and moist.
My dad burst out laughing. My mom looked amused.
Her Chapstick was lost. That was lipstick I'd used.

Computer Boot

When I powered my computer on today
it wouldn't boot,
so I tapped it just a little
but it still would not compute.

So I thumped a little harder
hoping that would make it go.
When it didn't help, I hit it with
an even bigger blow.

Then I punched it half a dozen times
which wasn't very smart,
for my knuckles hurt like heck
but my computer didn't start.

So I whacked it with a hammer
and I knocked it over flat,
and I probably should not have clubbed it
with my baseball bat.

But at least I needn't fret about
it booting anymore,
since I booted my computer
down the stairs and out the door.

My Pig Won't Let Me Watch TV

My pig won't let me watch TV.
It's totally unfair.
He watches anything he wants
but doesn't ever share.

I never get to watch cartoons
or anything like that.
He's busy watching farming shows.
I should have bought a cat.

I should have bought a goldfish
or a guinea pig or goat.
Instead, I've got this pig
who's always hogging the remote.

Halloween is Nearly Here

Halloween is nearly here.
I've got my costume planned.
It's sure to be the most horrific
outfit in the land.

If you should see me coming
you may scream and hide your head.
My get-up will, I guarantee,
fill every heart with dread.

My costume may cause nightmares.
Yes, my mask may stop your heart.
You might just shriek and wet yourself,
then squeamishly depart.

And yet, I won't be dressing as
you might expect me to.
I will not be a vampire
or ghost that hollers "boo!"

I won't look like a werewolf
or a goblin or a ghoul,
or even like a slimy blob
of deadly, dripping drool.

I will not be a zombie
or some other horrid creature.
No, this year I'll be much, much worse...
I'm dressing as a teacher.

Nimrod Nero, Superhero

Nimrod Nero, superhero,
never saves the day.
He doesn't fly.
He's known to cry.
He always runs away.

He doesn't have a cape and tights.
He doesn't own a mask.
He has no cool
belt or tool
to help with any task.

He isn't strong or fearless,
or impervious to pain.
He's slower than
a speeding bullet,
weaker than a train.

He couldn't leap a Barbie Playhouse
in a single bound.
He'll stay inside
his room and hide
when bad guys are around.

He doesn't laugh at danger
and he never battles crime.
He's only known
to sob and moan
and whimper all the time.

The world is so much safer now,
I think it's fair to say,
since Nimrod Nero,
superhero,
never saves the day.

I Tried to Catch a Snowflake

I tried to catch a snowflake.
I opened up my mouth.
Next year I think I'll wait until
the birds have all flown south.

Bloome the Human Boomerang

I'm Bloome, the human boomerang.
I soar up in the sky.
My skill is quite remarkable.
It's fun to watch me fly.

To start, I grab my ankles
and I lift me off the ground,
then swing myself in circles
till I'm spinning 'round and 'round.

And when I'm spinning fast enough
I say a little prayer,
then heave myself with all my might
and launch me in the air.

I fly a giant circle
and return right back to me.
Except today I missed and now
I'm stuck up in a tree.

I'm Clever Whenever

I'm clever whenever
there's no one around.
Alone, on my own,
I profess I'm profound.

In private, I'm Einstein.
Secluded, I'm smart.
My genius increases
the more I'm apart.

If you think I'm clueless,
it isn't a trick.
When people are present
I'm dumb as a brick.

But don't think I'm daft
or not mentally sound.
Whenever I'm clever
there's no one around.

My Birthday's On St. Patrick's Day

My birthday's on St. Patrick's day.
I wore no green at all,
and got a pinch from every kid
who passed me in the hall.
You get "a pinch to grow an inch"
whenever birthdays fall.
I guess they must have worked
because I'm thirty-nine feet tall.

I'm Not Afraid of the Dark

Oh, I'm not afraid of the darkness.
I don't mind an absence of light.
I can't say I'm scared of the sunset
or things that go "bump" in the night.

I've never been frightened of monsters
or tentacles under my bed.
Not skeletons, witches or goblins
or creatures come back from the dead.

I'm not at all worried of werewolves,
or even a vampire's bite.
I'm simply not scared of the darkness,
except when you turn off the light.

Breakfast in Bed

This morning I made my mom breakfast in bed.
I tried to be careful, but burnt all the bread.
I tried to make sure that the coffee was hot,
by boiling the bit left in yesterday's pot.

I charred a few pancakes, potatoes, and grits.
The sausage, I seared into smoldering bits.
I made her some muffins like miniature coals,
and roasted a package of cinnamon rolls.

I scorched several servings of hamburger hash,
and microwaved bacon until it was ash.
I blackened a bagel, which started to smoke.
The smoke alarm sounded. My mother awoke.

I think she was panicked. Her eyes filled with dread.
I proudly presented her breakfast in bed.
She grimaced, then silently counted to ten,
and asked me to never make breakfast again.

I Listen to My Chicken

I listen to my chicken
as she sings her cheerful song.
I'm tickled with my turkey
as he gobbles right along.

My duck sings so delightfully.
I love my rooster's rap,
and when my Cornish game hen croons
it makes me want to clap.

I give my goose a gander
and I giggle as she chimes,
for when it comes to poultry
I prefer the kind that rhymes.

Auntie Gravity

My sweet old Auntie Gravity
bakes all the lightest cakes.
Her "Secret X" ingredient
is all it ever takes.

A single splash of Secret X
provides her pies a lift.
A smidgen more and suddenly
her doughnuts are adrift.

A pinch upon her pancakes
and they rise above the plate.
A dash will make her danishes
begin to levitate.

Her muffins start to hover
from the tiniest of specks.
Her bagels float and flutter
when she uses Secret X.

But, sadly, Auntie Gravity
is known to make mistakes,
and may have used a bit too much
in several pies and cakes.

She ate a plate of chocolate cake
and tried a slice of mince.
I miss my Auntie Gravity;
we haven't seen her since.

My Mother Was a Hippie

My mother was a hippie.
My father was a punk.
And that is why
it happened I
turned out to be a hunk.

The Man from Timbuktu

I'll tell you of a man I knew
who claimed he came from Timbuktu.
He said, "I have the world to see!"
So off he went to Timbukthree.
Then Timbukfour and Timbukfive
were where he seemed to come alive.

He went to Timbuksix and -seven,
and Timbukeight, -nine, -ten, -eleven.
Then Timbuktwelve and -thirteen too,
he liked them more than Timbuktu.
The last I heard, he's doing fine.
He lives in Timbukninetynine.

So, kids, if all you ever do
is take a trip to Timbuktu,
at least you'll have a lot more fun
than staying home in Timbukone.
But if you have the world to see...
continue on to Timbukthree.

I Dreamed That There Were Dragons

I dreamed that there were dragons
on an island in the sea,
where they threw a raging party
and, of course, invited me.

They wanted me to celebrate
their dragon holiday,
so I learned the dragon disco
and we danced the night away.

It wasn't long at all before
I found that I could fly
as my flashing wings and flaming breath
lit up the midnight sky.

I soared with all the dragons
spinning circles overhead
till, at last, the party ended
and I made my way to bed.

You may not ever dream like this;
most people never do,
but *I* dream of dragons every night
for I'm a dragon too.

How Did You Get So Mean?

I caught you stealing second base.
I saw you killing time.
I know you shot some basketballs
and even flipped a dime.

I heard you cut some corners.
You were swinging at the park.
I saw you punch the clock
while stabbing blindly in the dark.

I watched you beat a dozen eggs.
I saw you strike a match.
You almost hit a hole-in-one.
I heard you slam the hatch.

You said you kicked the habit.
You got to crown the queen.
And now you want to break the news?
How did you get so mean?

Belinda Brooks

Belinda Brooks
loved library books,
She hoarded them all for herself.
She'd check them out
to spread them about
or straighten them up on a shelf.

She boxed her books
in crannies and nooks.
She filled every crevice and crack.
She stuffed her home
with textbook and tome
but never would take any back.

Her dresser drawer
held novels galore.
She kept them in cases and cans,
with lots and lots
in packets and pots,
and packages, parcels and pans.

She cleaned and wiped
the volumes she swiped,
and tenderly treasured each book.
She'd sit for days
and lovingly gaze
at all the editions she took.

In bowls and bins
and baskets and tins,
in canisters, cartons and crates,
so poor Miss Brooks,
with all of those books,
was wanted in fifty-two states.

For she was fined,
but always declined
to pay or surrender the books.
And so, in shame,
Belinda became
the biggest of library crooks.

When she got nailed,
Belinda was jailed
and sentenced to years for her deed.
So now, with time
for pay for her crime,
she's finally learning to read.

Brand New Shoes

I bought a brand new pair of shoes.
You simply have to see.
They're purple, pink, and pretty.
They're as lovely as can be.

They're topped with silver sparkles,
so they shimmer in the sun.
They're awesome when I'm walking
and they're stunning when I run.

The laces look like rainbows
and the backs have flashing lights.
The sides are lined with lightning bolts.
They're such amazing sights.

But now my friends avoid me
when they see me on the street.
Indeed, my shoes are pretty
but they smell like stinky feet.

A Reindeer for Christmas

Dear Santa, this Christmas my list is quite small.
In fact, I need practically nothing at all.
My list is so short and so easy to read
because there's just one thing I actually need.

A reindeer for Christmas is all I require;
a reindeer, of course, who's an excellent flier.
I really don't care if it's Dasher or Dancer.
I'm okay with Cupid or Comet or Prancer.

Please don't think I'm greedy; I only want one.
You won't even miss him, and I'll have such fun.
I promise I'll feed him and treat him just right,
and take him out flying around every night.

You see, I'm not selfish. So for my surprise
this Christmas, please bring me a reindeer that flies.
But if my request is a bit much for you,
I guess that an iPod will just have to do.

Here is the House

Here is the house
on the street in the town
where the downstairs is up
and the upstairs is down.

The people who live here
all stand on their heads.
They sleep on the ceilings
and can't reach their beds.

The basement's the attic.
The roof is the floor.
They climb up a ladder
to crawl through the door.

Their pets run in circles
because they're all dizzy.
This house is confusing
and everyone's busy.

The downstairs is upstairs.
The upstairs is down
since twenty tornadoes
blew into the town.

Hap-the-Happy-Hyphenator

I'm-Hap-the-Happy-Hyphenator.
Hyphens-are-my-thing.
I-like-the-way-they-give-my-words-
that-extra-bit-of-zing.

I-really-can't-explain-it,-
but-it-makes-me-feel-just-great.
And-so,-no-matter-what-I-write,
I-always-hyphenate.

I-do-not-like-parentheses.
Quotation-marks-are-dull.
Apostrophes-and-colons-drive-me-
right-out-of-my-skull.

I-do-not-need-the-angle-bracket,
question-mark-or-slash.
I'd-love-to-stay-and-tell-you-more-
but-now-I-have-to-dash-----

When Daniel Went Dancing

When Daniel went dancing that night at the fair
he leapt on the stage with his arms in the air.
He ran back and forth at a neck-breaking pace,
then back-flipped and cartwheeled all over the place.
He jumped like a jumping bean, bounced like a ball,
careened off the ceiling, and ran down the wall.

He flew through the room with an ear-splitting scream
till, shaking and sobbing, he ran out of steam.
The witnesses watching could see at a glance
that Dan had invented some new kind of dance.
They cheered and applauded. They gave him First Prize.
They cried, "You're a genius in all of our eyes!"
So now, just like Daniel, from Finland to France
they sit on a cactus to start every dance.

I Wrote This Little Poem

I wrote this little poem.
It was so much fun to write
that I scribbled through the afternoon,
the evening, and the night.
When the morning sun was rising
and the sky was growing light,
I went searching for some breakfast
but no breakfast was in sight.
(If you've ever needed breakfast
then you'll understand my plight.)

I was feeling fairly famished
so, although it isn't right,
I picked up this little poem
and I took a tiny bite.
It was utterly delicious!
It was such a sheer delight
that I nibbled through the afternoon,
the evening, and the night.
When the morning sun was rising
and the sky was growing light,
I went searching for this poem
but no poem was in sight.
So I wrote it down again and
it was so much fun to write
that I scribbled through the afternoon,
the evening, and the night.
If you think you know what happened next,
I think you may be right.

School Year Extension

I know it's the last day of school
but, students, I've thought of a way
that we can remain here together
a little bit longer today.

I hope you approve of my plan
for giving this year an extension.
Yes, students, I like you so much,
I'm putting you all in detention.

I Made a Hat

I made a hat from fur and felt,
a feather, and a leather belt.
I topped it with a pretty bow
and lots of ribbons, just for show.
I held it up, admiring it,
then tried it on. It wouldn't fit!
I pushed and pulled with all my might,
the front, the back, the left, the right.
And yet, no matter how I tried
it wouldn't fit. I nearly cried!
I yanked it off and yelped because
I saw then what the problem was.
I'm such a dolt, I had to frown.
I'd made the darned thing upside down!

Bad Bertie Bartigan

When Bad Bertie Bartigan came into town,
he held up the bank and his britches fell down.
"Dad gum it!" he spluttered. "Gawl durn it! Aw, shoot!"
then picked up his britches, but fumbled the loot.
He lit out of town in a mad-scramble dash.
He still had his pants, but he'd lost all the cash.

The stagecoach was passing that moment, by chance.
He held up the stagecoach, and down went his pants.
"Dag nab it!" he blurted. "Dad blame it! Aw, no!"
then hoisted his trousers, but dropped all the dough.
He ran for the hills with his britches held high,
but Bertie was broke and he wanted to cry.

And, as he was running, he spotted a train,
so Bertie, who wasn't renowned for his brain,
said, "This is a hold up!" His pants hit the deck.
"Garsh dang it!" he stammered. "Dog gone it. Aw, heck."
He ran away clutching his britches again,
straight into the sheriff and all of his men.

They busted Bad Bertie and tossed him in jail,
to wait for his sentence with no chance of bail.
And, there in the hoosegow, in handcuffs and chains,
he held up no bank tellers, coaches, or trains.
"Dad blast it! Tarnation! Aw, Sam Hill!" he said,
and stood there and held up his britches instead.

Recipe for Disaster

A box of melted crayons.
A cup of Elmer's glue.
A pint of watercolor paint.
Some Silly Putty too.

A half a pound of Playdough.
About a pint of paste.
A tablespoon of flubber
to improve the final taste.

I looked through all the cupboards
for things I could include.
If it was marked "Non-Toxic"
I just figured that meant "food."

To guarantee it's healthy
I topped it with a beet.
Then smashed it all together
so it should be good to eat.

I'm hoping that you'll try it
and tell me what you think.
Just close your eyes and open wide
and never mind the stink.

Our Family Picnic

My family went out on a picnic.
We lugged all our stuff to the park.
As soon as we'd spread out our blanket
it promptly got rainy and dark.

And while we were watching our napkins
and plates blow away in the breeze,
we all got attacked by mosquitoes
and plagued and tormented by bees.

Our sodas were slurped up by insects.
Our burgers were eaten by ants
which, once they were done with our lunches,
decided to crawl up our pants.

We couldn't hold out any longer.
We ran screaming madly away
and left all our stuff to the insects
and rain that had ruined our day.

So next time we'll go to the movies,
or maybe just go to the mall.
That last time we went on a picnic
was really no picnic at all.

My Grandpa

I'll tell you a bit of my grandpa.
I think he's a thousand years old.
He must keep his hands in the freezer;
I've never felt ice cubes that cold.

The hair growing off of his earlobes
is more than the hair on his head.
His eyes are all baggy and bloodshot.
His nose is the same shade of red.

His voice is like rickety floorboards.
It crackles and groans when he speaks.
Whenever he bends down to hug me
it sounds like his skeleton creaks.

He says that his memory is failing.
He thinks that he's losing his mind.
He's always misplacing his glasses;
without them he's legally blind.

My mom says his hearing is normal.
I kind of believe her, but then
whenever I tell him "I love you,"
he asks me to say it again.

Index

ABOUT THE AUTHOR

Kenn Nesbitt is the author of many books for children, including *The Ultimate Top Secret Guide to Taking Over the World*, *More Bears!*, *The Tighty-Whitey Spider*, and *My Hippo Has the Hiccups*. He is also the creator of the world's most popular children's poetry website, www.poetry4kids.com.

More Books by Kenn Nesbitt

I'm Growing a Truck in the Garden – Follow one boy through his day as he plays with his friends and creates havoc along the way. Collins Educational. ISBN: 978-0007462001.

The Ultimate Top Secret Guide to Taking Over the World – Are you fed up with people telling you what to do? You're in luck. All you have to do is read this book and carefully follow the instructions, and in no time at all you will be laughing maniacally as the world cowers before you. Sourcebooks Jabberwocky. ISBN: 978-1402238345.

MORE BEARS! – Kenn Nesbitt's picture book debut will have you laughing while shouting "More Bears!" along with the story's disruptive audience. The author/narrator keeps adding more and more bears, which he describes in humorous detail, until he gets fed up! The bears ride, dance, surf, and even somersault off the page. Sourcebooks Jabberwocky. ISBN: 978-1402238352.

The Tighty-Whitey Spider: And More Wacky Animals Poems I Totally Made Up – Following up the bestselling collection, *My Hippo Has the Hiccups*, Kenn Nesbitt dares to go where no poet has gone before. With poems like and "I Bought Our Cat a Jetpack" and "My Dog Plays Invisible Frisbee," this collection shines bright with rhymes that are full of jokes, thrills, and surprises. Sourcebooks Jabberwocky. ISBN: 978-1402238338.

My Hippo Has the Hiccups: And Other Poems I Totally Made Up - *My Hippo Has the Hiccups* contains over one hundred of Kenn's newest and best-loved poems. The dynamic CD brings the poems to life with Kenn reading his own poetry, cracking a joke or two, and even telling stories about how the poems came to be. Sourcebooks Jabberwocky. ISBN: 978-1402218095.

Revenge of the Lunch Ladies: The Hilarious Book of School Poetry – From principals skipping school to lunch ladies getting back at kids who complain about cafeteria food, school has never been so funny. Meadowbrook Press. ISBN: 978-1416943648.

When the Teacher Isn't Looking: And Other Funny School Poems – *When the Teacher Isn't Looking* may be the funniest collection of poems about school ever written. This collection of poems by Kenn Nesbitt is sure to have you in stitches from start to finish. Meadowbrook Press. ISBN: 978-0684031286.

The Aliens Have Landed at Our School – No matter what planet you live on, this book is packed with far-out, funny, clever poems guaranteed to give you a galactic case of the giggles. Meadowbrook Press. ISBN: 978-0689048647.

For more funny poems, visit
www.poetry4kids.com

Made in the USA
Middletown, DE
15 August 2015